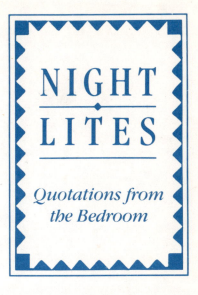

NIGHT LITES

Quotations from the Bedroom

Compiled by
Susie Teltser-Schwarz

Illustrated by
Michel Design

PETER PAUPER PRESS, INC.
WHITE PLAINS · NEW YORK

Copyright © 1989
Peter Pauper Press, Inc.
202 Mamaroneck Avenue
White Plains, NY 10601
ISBN 0-88088-449-5
Library of Congress No. 88-63475
Printed in the United States of America

Contents

Sex 5

Bed............................... 21

Sleep 33

Dreams 45

Insomnia.......................... 50

Limericks and Poetry............... 57

Sex

Last night I discovered a new form of oral contraceptive. I asked a girl to go to bed with me and she said no.
Woody Allen

Some things are better than sex, and some things are worse, but there's nothing exactly like it.
W. C. Fields

Sex is an emotion in motion.
Mae West

The big difference between sex for money and sex for free is that sex for money usually costs a lot less.
Brendan Francis

Sex is dirty only when it's done right.
>*Woody Allen*

A survey was taken on the nocturnal habits of men. The results showed that 5 percent of the men get up to drink a glass of water, 10 percent to go to the bathroom, and 85 percent get up to go home.
>*Joe Uris*

Three Frenchmen were trying to define *savoir-faire*. "If I go home," said Alphonse, "and find my wife sleeping with another man, say 'Excuse me' and leave, that is *savoir-faire*." "No," said Gaston, "if I go home and find my wife with another man, and say 'Excuse me, please continue,' that is *savoir-faire*." "*Au contraire*," said Pierre, "if I go home and find my wife with another man and say 'Excuse me, please continue,' and he *can* continue, then *he* has *savoir-faire*."

I'm a practicing heterosexual . . . but bisexuality immediately doubles your chances for a date on Saturday night.
Woody Allen

I don't know what I am, dahling. I've tried several varieties of sex. The conventional position makes me claustrophobic. And the others either give me a stiff neck or lockjaw.
Tallulah Bankhead

Whoever named it necking was a poor judge of anatomy.
Groucho Marx

Recall the old story of the rather refined young man who preferred sex dreams to visiting brothels because he met a much nicer type of girl that way.
Vivian Mercier

Six things not to say in bed:
Are you *sure* you have one?
Sorry, where were we?
Eric, can I call you back in about five minutes? Something has just cropped up with Thelma.
There's another crack in the ceiling.
Do you think it's a boil? Or could it be a carbuncle? Take a closer look.
I *know* I'm driving you mad with lust, but do you think we should have the walls rag-rolled in Sea Haze, with an aquamarine cornice and a white festoon blind or . . .
New Woman, London

Suburban Husband: a gardener with sex privileges
More Playboy's Party Jokes

If God had meant us to have group sex, he'd have given us more organs.
Malcolm Bradbury

Woman, observing that her mate went out of his way to make himself entertaining, rightly surmised that sex had something to do with it. From that she logically concluded that sex was recreational rather than procreational. (The small hardy band of girls who failed to get this point were responsible for the popularity of women's field hockey.)
> *James Thurber and E. B. White*

Sex is too often not only Topic A, but also Topics B and C as well.
> *Time,* on John O'Hara's writing

Sex—the poor man's polo.
> *Clifford Odets*

Rare are they who prefer virtue to the pleasures of sex.
> *Confucius*

The reason people sweat is so they won't catch fire when making love.
Don Rose

Whatever else can be said about sex, it cannot be called a dignified performance.
Helen Lawrenson

The love game is never called off on account of darkness.
Tom Masson

When the candles are out all women are fair.
Plutarch

It used to be you'd be embarrassed to get condoms, but buying cigarettes was O.K. Now it's O.K. to get *condoms,* but you're embarrassed to buy *cigarettes!*
          Jackie Mason

I can only tell you his Who's Who is six inches long.
        Minnie Guggenheim,
   introducing a prominent political figure

The trouble with incest is that it gets you involved with relatives.
         George S. Kaufman

There is no economy in going to bed early to save candles if the result is twins.
         Chinese Proverb

The same kind of women who used to insist they were virgins now go around insisting that they're insatiable, and we're still lying about sex as much as ever.
Judith Viorst

Lord give me chastity—but not yet.
Saint Augustine

Why does a man use a "camouflage" condom?
So you can't see him coming.

The brain is viewed as an appendage of the genital glands.
Dr. Carl Jung

Is it not strange that desire should so many years outlive performance?
Shakespeare

Don't knock it, it's sex with someone you love.
Woody Allen, on masturbation

Men always fall for frigid women because they put on the best show.
Fanny Brice

Continental people have sex life; the English have hot-water bottles.
George Mikes

There is no greater nor keener pleasure than that of bodily love—and none which is more irrational.

Plato

Literature is mostly about having sex and not much about having children; life is the other way round.

John Davis Lodge

It has to be admitted that we English have sex on the brain, which is a very unsatisfactory place to have it.

Malcolm Muggeridge

It was the most fun I ever had without laughing.

Woody Allen, on sex

A husband and wife were relaxing in their bedroom after attending their 45th wedding anniversary party. Suddenly, the wife got up and, without warning, slapped her husband across the face. "That," she said, "is for 45 years of lousy sex."

The husband sat thoughtfully for a few moments, then rose and slapped his wife across the face. "And that," he said, "is for knowing the difference!"

Of the delights of this world man cares most for sexual intercourse, yet he has left it out of his heaven.
Mark Twain

Sex: One of the nine reasons for reincarnation ... the other eight are unimportant.
Henry Miller

Never go to bed with a woman whose troubles are greater than your own.
Nelson Algren

Litigation takes the place of sex at middle age.

Gore Vidal

All this fuss about sleeping together. For physical pleasure I'd sooner go to the dentist any day.

Evelyn Waugh

Communication, separate bedrooms and separate baths.

Bette Davis, on what makes a marriage work

Only the nose knows
Where the nose goes
When the door close.

Muhammad Ali, when asked what he thought about a fighter having sex the night before a big fight

After couples are married for a while they tend to take sex for granted. They don't even bother to lock the door. Big mistake. Sex has to be behind locked doors. If what you're doing can be done out in the open, you might as well be pitching horseshoes.
George Burns

Sex is the great amateur art. The professional, male or female, is frowned on; he or she misses the whole point and spoils the show.
David Cort

Love is not the dying moan of a distant violin—it's the triumphant twang of a bedspring.
S. J. Perelman

It doesn't matter what you do in the bedroom as long as you don't do it in the street and frighten the horses.
Mrs. Patrick Campbell

I have to be honest. I was a lousy lover. But Gracie married me for laughs, not for sex. Of course she got both of them—when we had sex, she laughed.

George Burns

Sex may be a hallowing and renewing experience, but more often it will be distracting, coercive, playful, frivolous, discouraging, dutiful and even boring.

Leslie H. Farber

When he's late for dinner, I know he's either having an affair or is lying dead in the street. I always hope it's the street.

Jessica Tandy, on her husband, Hume Cronyn

Outercourse is a lot less intimate than intercourse, but safer. Any further course is up to you!

Susie Teltser-Schwarz

Bed

More belongs to marriage than four bare legs in a bed.

The best time for parents to put the children to bed is while they still have the strength.
Homer Phillips

Never go to bed mad. Stay up and fight.
Phyllis Diller

My wife probably feels that our bed has become a G movie, but I am actually in tune with the times, for recent surveys have revealed that most women would rather cuddle than have sex, and I am the Clark Gable of cuddlers.

Bill Cosby

Wedlock—The deep, deep peace of the double bed after the hurly-burly of the chaise-longue.
> *Mrs. Patrick Campbell*

No bed is big enough to hold three.
> *German Proverb*

Early to bed and early to rise, and you'll meet very few of our best people.
> *George Ade*

Why did the moron take hay to bed?
He wanted to feed his night mare.

Bundling was an old New England tradition
introduced by the Dutch and the English
which permitted engaged couples to lie
together in bed without undressing during
long, cold winter evenings.

Mark Ishee

Bed is the best place for reading, thinking, or
doing nothing.

Doris Lessing

You make your bed and you must lie on it.

Charles Dickens

For I've been born and I've been wed—
All of man's peril comes of bed.

C. H. Webb

Item, I give unto my wife my second best bed.

> *William Shakespeare,*
> bequest in his will

We can heat the body, we can cool it; we can give it tension or relaxation; and surely it is possible to bring it into a state in which rising from bed will not be a pain.

> *James Boswell*

Wanted: Playpen, cot and highchair. Also two single beds.

> *Advertisement in* Evening Standard

The actor rushes from the bed to the altar almost as fast as other men rush from the altar to the bed.

> *H. L. Mencken*

What a delightful thing rest is!—The bed has become a place of luxury to me.—I would not exchange it for all the thrones in the world.

Napoleon

I must marry—if only to get to bed at a reasonable hour.

Benjamin Constant

The bed is a bundle of paradoxes: we go to it with reluctance, yet we quit it with regret; we make up our minds every night to leave it early, but we make up our bodies every morning to keep it late.

Colton

The only man who can take a nap on top of a bedspread is a bachelor.

The persons hardest to convince they're at the retirement age are children at bedtime.
Shannon Fife

Twin beds became popular when men began to realize they should not take their troubles to bed with them.

That bed was on fire when I got into it.
Rudy York, when accused by a hotel manager of starting a fire by smoking in bed

Children never put off until tomorrow that which will keep them out of bed tonight.
Glen Preston Burns

Quilt Guilt: Always hogging more than your share of the covers.
Judith Viorst

Attitude is all-important. When you're around my age you've got to keep occupied. You've got to do something that will get you out of bed. I never made a nickel in bed. Yeah, get out of bed. Find something that will make you do it—like an interest . . . a hobby . . . a business . . . a pretty girl—there we are back in bed again.
George Burns

The only interesting thing that can happen in a Swiss bedroom is suffocation by a feather mattress.
Dalton Trumbo

No civilized person ever goes to bed the same day he gets up.
Richard Harding Davis

How it is I know not; but there is no place like a bed for confidential disclosures between friends. Man and wife, they say, there open the very bottom of their souls to each other; and some old couples often lie and chat over old times till nearly morning.
Herman Melville

Early to bed and early to rise is a sure sign that you don't care for television.

If a bed would tell all it knows, it would put many to the blush.
English Proverb

The bed is the best rendevou[s] of mankind, and the most necessary ornament of a chamber.
Sir Thomas Overbury

Bed is often the place where you see the funny side of marriage. It is also the place where you can be offended, furious or just downright disappointed when the lights are off.
Laurie Graham

To do each day two things one dislikes is a precept I have followed scrupulously; every day I have got up and I have gone to bed.
William Somerset Maugham

The happiest part of a man's life is what he passes lying awake in bed in the morning.
Dr. Samuel Johnson

Last week we passed a birth-control bill. Now we are trying to pass a law to put the people to bed an hour earlier.
Frank L. Gill,
on daylight-saving time legislation

A man of sixty has spent twenty years in bed
and over three years in eating.
                              Arnold Bennett

Rather go to bed supperless than rise in
debt.
                              Ben Franklin

Woe to them that work evil upon their beds.
              Old Testament. Micah 2:1

The only perfect climate is bed.
                         Frank Crowninshield

Better a bed of wood than a bier of gold.
Russian Proverb

Republicans sleep in twin beds—some even in separate rooms. That is why there are more Democrats.
Will Stanton

Bed springs eternal!
Susie Teltser-Schwarz

We stand behind every bed we sell.
Advertisement for Kleinsleep

Sleep

The average, healthy, well-adjusted adult gets up at seven-thirty in the morning feeling just plain terrible.

Jean Kerr

Before marriage, a man will lie awake all night thinking about something you said; after marriage, he'll fall asleep before you finish saying it.

Helen Rowland

People who say they sleep like a baby usually don't have one.

Leo J. Burke

The gent who wakes up and finds himself a success hasn't been asleep.

Addison Mizner

A good husband is never the first to go to sleep at night or the last to awake in the morning.

Honoré de Balzac

The preacher mumbled a few words in his throat and they were married. A few months later the husband mumbled a few words in his sleep and they were divorced.

Mildred Meiers and Jack Knapp

I wake up every morning at nine and grab for the morning paper, Then I look at the obituary page. If my name is not on it, I get up.

Harry Hershfield

A man is almost always ridiculous when he is asleep.

Honoré de Balzac

Maybe it's because I sleep slow.
> *Jack Teagarden,* explaining why
> he liked to sleep so long

What can you expect of a day that begins with getting up in the morning?
> *Farmer's Almanac, 1966*

Was it true, as legend had it, that Mr. Edison, like Napoleon, slept but four hours? Yes, said Mr. Ford, but Mr. Edison slept twice and sometimes three times a day!
> *Gene Fowler*

"A man ought to have more than just two sides to sleep on," declared Simple. "Now if I get tired of sleeping on my left side, I have nothing to turn over on but my right side."
> *Langston Hughes*

Discipline is not as simple nor as easy as it might appear. A little girl said to her father, "I don't think mama knows much about bringing up children." The father asked, "Why?" The little girl replied, "Well, she makes me go to bed when I'm not sleepy and makes me get up when I am sleepy."
Perry F. Webb

The best bait for bedbugs is to sleep three in a bed.
Josh Billings

It is not easy for Catholics and Protestants to lie in the same bed, unless both are asleep.
William Ralph Inge

I always think a bed that hasn't been slept in looks sort of forlorn in the morning.
John van Druten

The vigorous are no better than the lazy during one half of life, for all men are alike when asleep.
Aristotle

Even back in Grandpa's time there was something to make you sleep. They called it work.

I dreamed last night of Clark Gable. He held me in his arms and then he hugged me and kissed me.
Then what happened?
It was time to get up—but I'm going to bed early this evening.
Mildred Meiers and Jack Knapp

Snoring—the tuneful serenade of that wakeful nightingale, the nose.
George Farquhar

Sleep: an eight-hour peep show of infantile erotica
> *J. G. Ballard*

To sleep, perchance to dream; ay, there's the rub;
For in that sleep of death what dreams may come,
When we have shuffled off this mortal coil,
Must give us pause.
> *William Shakespeare,* Hamlet

The sleep of a labouring man is sweet.
> *Old Testament. Ecclesiastes 5:12*

Sleep is the best cure for waking troubles.
> *Cervantes*

Hotel Clerk: (To guest parading through lobby in pajamas) "Here, what are you doing?"
Guest: (Awakened) "Beg pardon! I'm a somnambulist."
Hotel Clerk: "Well, you can't walk around here like that, no matter what your religion is."

Mildred Meiers and Jack Knapp

He who sleeps in continual noise is wakened by silence.

William Dean Howells

Good night. Sleep tight. Don't let the bedbugs bite.

Jake Falstaff

Sleeping is no mean art. For its sake one must stay awake all day.
Friedrich Nietzsche

That we are not much sicker and much madder than we are is due exclusively to that most blessed and blessing of all natural graces, sleep.
Aldous Huxley

Sleep faster, we need the pillows.
Jewish Proverb

I went for the first time into a naked bed, only my drawers on; and did sleep pretty well.
Samuel Pepys

I fell asleep reading a dull book and dreamed
I kept on reading, so I awoke from sheer
boredom.
Heinrich Heine

There is only one thing people like that is
good for them: a good night's sleep.
Ed Howe

Well enough for old folks to rise early,
because they have done so many mean things
all their lives they can't sleep anyhow.
Mark Twain

No man should ever lose sleep over *public
affairs.*
Harold Macmillan

Sleep falls like silence on the earth, it fills the hearts of ninety million men, it moves like magic in the mountains, and walks like night and darkness across the plains and rivers of the earth, until low upon lowlands, and high upon hills, flows gently sleep, smooth-sliding sleep—oh, sleep—sleep—sleep!
Thomas Wolfe

One hour's sleep before midnight is worth three after.
George Herbert

Sleep is the poor man's treasure.
Latvian Proverb

Fatigue is the best pillow.
Benjamin Franklin

I know a couple who talk in their sleep. He plays golf, and she loves to go to auction sales. The other night the golfer yelled: "Fore!" And the wife yelled: "Four twenty-five!"
Mildred Meiers and Jack Knapp

In order to know when it is time to sleep I *never* look at my watch. I do that *only* mornings, to find out when it is time to get up.
Brahms

Not all are asleep who have their eyes shut.
Proverb

Not all with their eyes open are awake.
Arthur L. Schwarz

Dreams

I had a wonderful dream last night—don't miss it.
> *Groucho Marx*

Dream research is a wonderful field. All you do is sleep for a living.
> *Stephen LaBerge*

If a man wants his dreams to come true, he must wake up.

I had a dream about reality. It was such a relief to wake up.
> *Stanislaw J. Lec*

One of the most adventurous things left us is to go to bed. For no one can lay a hand on our dreams.

E. V. Lucas

We are such stuff
As dreams are made on, and our little life
Is rounded with a sleep.

Shakespeare, The Tempest

Dream: the theater where the dreamer is at once scene, actor, prompter, stage manager, author, audience, and critic.

Carl Jung

When we can't dream any longer we die.

Emma Goldman

We use up too much artistic effort in our dreams; in consequence our waking life is often poor.

Nietzsche

I like the dreams of the future better than the history of the past.

Thomas Jefferson

Your old men shall dream dreams, your young men shall see visions.

Old Testament. Joel 2:28

Anyone can escape into sleep, we are all geniuses when we dream, the butcher's the poet's equal there.

E. M. Cioran

The pleasure of the true dreamer does not lie in the substance of the dream, but in this: that there things happen without any interference from his side, and altogether outside his control.
Isak Dinesen, Out of Africa

Dreaming permits each and every one of us to be quietly and safely insane every night of our lives.
Dr. William Dement

May blessings light upon him who first invented sleep! It is food for the hungry, drink for the thirsty, heat for the cold, and cold for the hot. It is the coin that buys all things, and the balance that makes the king even with the shepherd, and the fool with the wise.
Cervantes

Insomnia

The best cure for insomnia is to get a lot of sleep.

W. C. Fields

I haven't been to sleep for over a year. That's why I go to bed early. One needs more rest if one doesn't sleep.

Evelyn Waugh

Insomnia is a gross feeder. It will nourish itself on any kind of thinking, including thinking about thinking.

Clifton Fadiman

Yes, I slept, but I dreamed that I didn't.
>> *Irving Berlin,* known as an
>> insomniac, when asked if he had
>> gotten any sleep the night before

Did you ever meet anyone who said he
couldn't sleep last night because of his
conscience?

The worst things:
To be in bed and sleep not,
To want for one who comes not,
To try to please and please not.
>> *Egyptian Proverb*

Sleep is as nice as woman,
The more I court it, the more it flies me.
>> *Sir John Suckling*

NIGHTMARE

When you're lying awake with a dismal
  headache, and repose is taboo'd by anxiety,
I conceive you may use any language you
  choose to indulge in, without impropriety;
For your brain is on fire—the bedclothes
  conspire of usual slumber to plunder you:
First your counterpane goes, and uncovers
  your toes, and your sheet slips demurely
  from under you;
Then the blanketing tickles—you feel like
  mixed pickles—so terribly sharp is the
  pricking,
And you're hot, and you're cross, and you
  tumble and toss till there's nothing 'twixt
  you and the ticking.
Then the bedclothes all creep to the ground
  in a heap, and you pick 'em all up in a
  tangle;
Next your pillow resigns and politely declines
  to remain at its usual angle!
Well, you get some repose in the form of a
  doze, with hot eye-balls and head ever
  aching,

But your slumbering teems with such horrible dreams that you'd very much better be waking;
   . . .
. . . you awake with a shudder despairing—
You're a regular wreck, with a crick in your neck, and no wonder you snore, for your head's on the floor, and you've needles and pins from your soles to your shins, and your flesh is a-creep for your left leg's asleep, and you've cramp in your toes, and a fly on your nose, and some fluff in your lung, and a feverish tongue, and a thirst that's intense, and a general sense that you haven't been sleeping in clover;
But the darkness has passed, and it's daylight at last, and the night has been long—ditto ditto my song—and thank goodness they're both of them over!

W. S. Gilbert, Iolanthe, Act II

What do you take as a remedy for your insomnia?
A glass of wine at regular intervals.
Does that make you sleep?
No, but it makes me content to stay awake.
Mildred Meiers and Jack Knapp

A woman who was divorcing her husband told the judge, "Your Honor, he swears at me in his sleep."

"That's a lie, your Honor," shouted the husband. "I'm not asleep!"
Myron Cohen

When a Congressman is trying to sleep, he counts his sheep in billions.

Sometimes a man can't sleep because he bought too much on the lay-awake plan.

How do people go to sleep? I'm afraid I've lost the knack. I might try busting myself smartly over the temple with the nightlight. I might repeat to myself, slowly and soothingly, a list of quotations beautiful from minds profound; if I can remember any of the damn things.

Dorothy Parker

Limericks and Poetry

The limerick's an art form complex
Whose contents run chiefly to sex;
   It's famous for virgins
   And masculine urgin's,
And vulgar erotic effects.

There was a young fellow in Maine
Who courted a girl all in vain;
   She cussed when he kissed her
   So he slept with her sister
Again and again and again!

If intercourse gives you thrombosis
While continence causes neurosis,
   I prefer to expire
   Fulfilling desire
Than live on in a state of psychosis.

A fox-hunting lady named Maud
At love was a terrible fraud;
   With the boys in the stable
   She was willing and able,
But in bed with her spouse she was bored.

Despite her impressive physique
Fatima was really quite meek;
   If a mouse showed its head,
   She would jump into bed
With a terrible blood-curdling sheik.

Wee Willie Winkie rins through the toun,
Upstairs and dounstairs, in his nichtgoun,
Tirlin' at the window, cryin' at the lock,
"Are the weans in their bed? for it's nou ten o'clock."

William Miller

A sleeper from the Amazon
Put nighties of his gra'mazon—
   The reason, that
   He was too fat
To get his own pajamazon.

Anonymous

The day is done, and the darkness
   Falls from the wings of Night,
As a feather is wafted downward
   From an eagle in his flight.

Henry Wadsworth Longfellow

Between the dark and the daylight,
   When the night is beginning to lower,
Comes a pause in the day's occupations,
   That is known as the Children's Hour.

Henry Wadsworth Longfellow

Once upon a midnight dreary, while I
  pondered, weak and weary,
Over many a quaint and curious volume
  of forgotten lore,
While I nodded, nearly napping, suddenly
  there came a tapping,
As of some one gently rapping, rapping at
  my chamber door.
" 'Tis some visitor," I muttered, "tapping at
  my chamber door—
  Only this and nothing more."

Edgar Allan Poe, The Raven

Now I lay me down to sleep,
I pray the Lord my soul to keep;
If I should die before I wake,
I pray the Lord my soul to take.

New England Primer

The night has a thousand eyes,
  And the day but one;
Yet the light of the bright world dies
  With the dying sun.

F. W. Bourdillon

Matthew, Mark, Luke, and John,
The Bed be blest that I lie on.
Four angels to my bed,
Four angels round my head,
One to watch, and one to pray,
And two to bear my soul away.

Thomas Ady

What a bliss to press the pillow
   Of a cottage-chamber bed
And to listen to the patter
   Of the soft rain overhead!

Coates Kinney

Come sleep! O sleep, the certain knot of
   peace,
The baiting place of wit, the balm of woe,
The poor man's wealth, the prisoner's release,
Th' indifferent judge between the high and
   low.

Sir Philip Sidney

In winter I get up at night
And dress by yellow candle-light.
In summer, quite the other way,—
I have to go to bed by day.

I have to go to bed and see
The birds still hopping on the tree,
Or hear the grown-up people's feet
Still going past me in the street.

And does it not seem hard to you,
When all the sky is clear and blue,
And I should like so much to play,
To have to go to bed by day?
Robert Louis Stevenson

Hush-a-bye, baby, on the tree-top,
When the wind blows, the cradle will rock;
When the bough breaks, the cradle will fall
And down will come baby, cradle, and all.
Anonymous

And the night shall be filled with music
    And the cares that infest the day,
Shall fold their tents like the Arabs,
    And as silently steal away.
Henry Wadsworth Longfellow

In bed we laugh, in bed we cry;
And, born in bed, in bed we die.
The near approach a bed may show
Of human bliss to human woe.
Isaac de Benserade